Blogging for Business

Amy Morse

Your step by step guide to setting the scene with a blog, then telling the story of your business.

Copyright © 2016 Amy Morse

All rights reserved.

ISBN: 1534798528
ISBN-13: 9781534798526

Linda

Rock your blog with these tips!

Amy xo

Acknowledgements

There are so many people to thank for helping me get this far with my business and my books.

Thanks to everyone who has read my blogs and followed my progress.
Thanks all the readers who have bought my books and supported my career as a writer, writing fiction as Amy C Fitzjohn and non-fiction as Amy Morse.

Thank you to Lidia Drzewiecka of Visuable and Gosia Scarrott of GS Styling for the great photoshoot to produce the images featured on the cover. Lidia's amazing skills as a marketer and photographer have resulted in a gorgeous set of pictures.

My biggest thanks goes to my fantastic, ever supportive, husband, Graham Morse, who produced the cover layout, helped with proofing and editing and who encourages me in everything I do.

CONTENTS

Introduction 6

Blogging: What's That All About? 8

Blogging: Why Do It? 9

The Pitfalls of Blogging 12

Tips for Beginners 13

Maintaining Momentum 18

Bringing It To Life 21

Anatomy of an Effective Blog Post 28

Be Inspired 29

Eyes On 34

Action Templates 36

More Books 40

About the Author 41

Introduction

First and foremost, I'm a story lover and a story teller. Stories are at the heart of everything I do; creating, shaping, sharing and drawing out stories.

In 2013, I fulfilled a lifelong dream by publishing my first novel (The Bronze Box, writing in my maiden name: Amy C Fitzjohn). Since then I've built a business around my love of stories, and my books.

With my background in skills training, business support and writing, I now work with small businesses, like you, to help them write their way to success.

You will always be the best narrator for the story of your business, and through my eBooks, workshops, 1:1 support and subscription services, I help you with the tools and confidence to tell the story of your business well, in your own words.

> "If we react, we act…"

I also work with business leaders and entrepreneurs who are writing a book to build authority in their business. If you have a book in you I can help draw it out.

Stories are how we learn; stories inspire, stories influence, stories move people – movement means action. We react, we act, and we do so on an emotional and empathetic level, it's how we connect to the world and shape our own space in it; it's how we build relationships and community. Since the dawn of time, sharing stories around a campfire, to our modern world of viral videos, inspiring images, brilliant blogs and sharable social strategy.

Stories are the secret to success; whatever success means to you (and it's different for all of us) because in business, people don't just buy people they buy stories.

I've been blogging for many years now; I love the immediacy of being published, getting valuable feedback and social proof.

I piloted my first 'Blogging for Business' workshop in my home city of Bristol, UK, in 2015. Since then I've grown, and I now deliver these workshops in small businesses to teams of staff, and for agencies working with startups.

> "In business, people don't just buy people they buy stories."

In this simple, step by step guide, I will share my knowledge and experience of using one of the most effective tools in your marketing toolbox to share your words with the world: Blogging.

I will guide you through what blogging is and why it is such a powerful way to share your message and build your authority as a business. I will share my writer's secrets and insights, get you fired up with a wealth of ideas for compelling content and give you some tools, tips and actionable strategies to build your business with a blog.

Blogging: What's That All About?

The term 'blog', was first coined in 1999 and evolved from 'weblog'.

Defined as:

> *A discussion or informational site published online consisting of discrete entries 'posts' typically displayed in reverse chronological order (most recent first). Commentary on a particular subject. Tool for outreach and opinion forming. Sharing information and influencing others.*
>
> *(Source: Wikipedia)*

In short, it's a way of recording the ongoing story of you and your business.

What started as a way for techies to share intelligence online in the early days of the internet, has become a global phenomenon.

According to 'digitalinformationworld.com' there are 240 million blogs, 82% of consumers enjoy reading blogs about their favourite brands and if your website has a blog it will attract 97% more traffic.

Some bloggers make a living from it. As with any business, if you intend to use your blog in of itself to make money, (for example, through paid advertising, recommending and reviewing products, etc.) you will need to be strategic about it and have some form of a business plan.

Although I will touch on ways to monetise your blog itself, the purpose of this book is to guide you in the use of your blog as a marketing tool for your wider business, whatever that may be. It could be your business as: a therapist, a baker, a stylist, a coach, a recruiter, a writer, a public speaker, an artist, an accountant, etc.– it doesn't matter; you know *your thing*, you are passionate about what you do and a blog is just another way to make money doing what you love.

Blogging is one of the simplest and most immediate ways to demonstrate your style, expertise and share knowledge.

Bloggers never run out of things to say on Social Media (essentially Social Media is just a form of micro blogging).

Blogging: Why Do It?

A blog that works well for your business takes time, commitment, energy and consistency. It can be difficult keeping up the momentum to take on such a challenge… it needs to be worth it.

The fact you have bought this book is an excellent start, and I have to assume you are at least interested on some level in blogging well to build your business. As with anything, the more knowledge and experience you have on a topic the easier it becomes to tackle.

Here are ten benefits to you and your business from blogging:

1. **Improve your writing**
   Being able to communicate effectively in writing is a key skill in business and in our digitally connected world.

2. **Focus**
   Keeping a blog allows you to develop some healthy habits such as; discipline, commitment and focus. You can process ideas, organise thoughts and concentrate on your priorities.

3. **Accountability**
   By writing in a public forum you are making a commitment to do something. If you say you're working on something on your blog, you feel a responsibility to actually do it and not get distracted.

4. **Research**
   Blogging gives you an excuse to research topics that fascinate you. It allows you to be a much more systematic and organised researcher. Pinterest is a useful tool to research, collect and curate information.

5. **Meeting new people**
   Blogging allows you to make connections in the virtual and real world space.

6. **Showcase others**
    Showcasing other people's content is a great way of acknowledging their expertise, creating a lasting connection with that person and increasing your own reach across other networks.

7. **Demonstrating my expertise**
    Looking back on your old content is a great confidence boost when you realise just how much knowledge and expertise you have in your subject. You can establish your credibility, expertise and build your brand.

8. **To be noticed**
    With thousands of new websites being created every day it's easy to get lost in the noise and chatter of the digital marketplace.

    Blogging keeps your web presence regular and consistent, helps with SEO*, keeps you immediate and adds value on social media - ultimately all of that helps sell products/services.

9. **Money**
    As you grow your blog you can help make it pay for the time you spend on it through affiliate links, adverts, paid downloads, eBooks and sponsorship, etc.

10. **Inspire and Influence**
    Again, this builds relationships, credibility and self-confidence. It's rewarding to know that you've made an impact.

In my workshops, I encourage discussion within the group on how they could benefit from blogging. Here's eleven more reasons to blog that have come out of my workshops:

1. Being concise

2. Show your human side – the person behind the picture

3. Personal journaling

4. Give people something to share

5. Sharing your journey

6. Therapeutic

7. Build a story

8. Create dialogue – opening and closing discussions

9. Grow your network and get to know others – be part of a community of bloggers

10. Something to include in newsletters

11. Something you can repurpose i.e. into an eBook or course materials, etc. (more on this later).

As an author, one of the most important ways that blogging has benefited me is the first on the list 'improve your writing'. Even in an increasingly visual digital space, with the growth of platforms such as Instagram and Pinterest, and the use of videos, words are still important.

Even if you 'Vlog' (Video Blog) you will need to describe what the video is about in writing so it can be discovered and shared, and likewise with images; for the image to be found there needs to be written description - 'Image 1' is not going to be found on Google!

A Word on SEO

SEO*, or 'Search Engine Optimization' is basically, getting your website to the top of Google.

When you distil it down, SEO is simply writing the right words, in the right place, in the right way, at the right time so content can be discovered and boosted up the search chain.

Having a blog on your website is the single biggest thing you can do to get your website a) noticed by Google as 'living' content and b) give potential customers a reason to hang around in your virtual shop, making them more likely to buy something.

Build a high quality website and a well written blog and SEO pretty much looks after itself!

The Pitfalls of Blogging

That all sounds great, doesn't it? But it's not all plain sailing, there are pitfalls to consider:

Setting Boundaries
While as businesses we want to show our human side, at the same time, we need to be mindful of setting some personal boundaries. We are not the same person at work as we are in our own time. This distinction can often be blurred when you work for yourself. Respect your own privacy, as you would anyone else's.

Be clear with yourself what you are prepared for strangers to know about you and what you don't want them to know.

If you must ask the question 'should I write that?' the answer is invariably 'no'!

Time
This is by far and away the biggest issue my clients share with me about blogging. We all have the same number of hours in a day and you are the master of your own destiny. As with anything, decide on your priorities, plan ahead and make time to do things that are important. Create some time in your schedule to write content, even if it's only a couple of hours a month, then build it into your routine.

What to say
We cover ideas later in this book but I recommend having a 'campaign' each month and making your content relevant to it. For example: if you have an event planned one month make that month's content all about the event.

Consistency
The only way to do something consistently is to plan it in. Even a loose plan; preferably written down. If a plan isn't written down, or recorded in some way, you probably won't do it; it will drift from your consciousness with everything else that isn't an immediate priority – until it becomes a priority (and by then it's often too late).

Tips for Beginners

Even if you are reading this book because you already have a blog and are looking to improve it, don't skip this section. Improvement always starts with getting the basics right. Is there something missing in the foundation of your blog that could be hurting you?

There are different ways you can venture into the world of blogging; you could use an online blogging platform such as blogger.com or you could host your blog on your website.

There are advantages and disadvantages to both.

If you are new to blogging, a good way to start could be to play around on the free online platforms for a while and when you get more comfortable and confident, then have your blog on your website.

However, ultimately, if you are using your blog to promote your business, build your brand authenticity and expertise in your sector, you will want to have your blog on your website, as that is the online 'shop window' for your business.

Here are my top tips for beginning bloggers:

Have a theme
Choose something that is appealing to your customers and have a consistent theme throughout. We're all interested in lots of topics, especially writers and creatives, we're naturally curious and observant, but the aim is to build a fan base and a following, not to get lots of people who are mildly interested in some of your stuff, then switch off and forget about you without buying your product/service. If you have a specialism, or a niche (always recommended) in your business, use it on your blog. If your business is pretty functional and hard to write interesting content about, think further and find a common theme that connects your customers. For example: if you sell insulation (yeah, not sexy) think about why people buy insulation?

- They want to save money on heating their home and they will probably be interested in the environment.

Perhaps you could have a theme on the latest innovations in green technology (much sexier)? The 'theme' doesn't necessarily need to be the product/service you sell; the important thing is the theme must be of interest to your target audience.

Blog regularly and consistently
Don't fall into the feast or famine trap – build blogging into your regular routines. For example: publish once a week on a Saturday. Once a month is a bare minimum - you don't have to blog daily (unless you really want to), and weekly is enough to keep people engaged.

Vary the content
Keep it interesting. Have videos, audio, words, images, lists, stories, tips, questionnaires, graphs, infographics, interviews, etc. There are so many different ways to present your information (see 'Be Inspired' chapter for more on this).

Reams of text on a blog gets stale very quickly. Break it up. Have plenty of whitespace. Make it bite sized and not too wordy. Keep it informal, friendly and accessible and people will come back for more.

Make it easily sharable
Make sure you have social media links on it. Make use of tools like 'click to tweet'. Create images that also have text on them, these are ideal for Pinterest, especially if your customers are woman - more women use Pinterest than any other social media platform.

Always include at least 1 image per post
Images have more impact on social media and are more likely to be shared. Also, it breaks up the look of the page making it easier on the eyes than just big blocks of text. As mentioned above, this makes your blog much more accessible for Pinterest. I (and millions of others) use Pinterest as a way to curate links and bookmark content online for future reference, there are few things as annoying as not being able to do that with a blog post because there is no image. People will go elsewhere to find content if they don't have a simple way to capture the link and store it for future reference.

Have a plan
Be organised. It's easy to publish content weekly if you know what to post, it's a nightmare if you are having to think on your feet all the time. It doesn't have to be complicated. Keep adding to the plan and try to stay a step ahead so that you're not in a panic trying to decide what to blog about.

Always include a Call to Action
A 'Call to Action' is giving the reader something to do next. It could be a link to an eBook, a link to book in for an event or appointment, an offer on a product in your shop, a 'click here for more information' link, etc. – once you have someone browsing your blog you want to convert them into a customer, the easier you make this for them the better the rate of success.

Do plenty of research
I find Pinterest invaluable for this. I have boards where I collect tips and ideas for blogging, I have boards for book research, I have boards for writing ideas and inspiration and I have boards of other curated links I can draw on. When I come to sit down and prepare some blog content, I have plenty of sources to draw on and my biggest challenge is what to choose next. It becomes a pleasurable experience, rather than a chore when you start to build up a repository of ideas you are desperate to share with people.

Invite contributions from others
It's a lovely thing to host someone else on your blog. It saves you having to write content for that 'episode', it builds relationships with others and it allows you to increase your reach by accessing other people's networks. It can be a bit of leg work to get people to do it, however, and sometimes you may have to chase people. Don't rely on it for your schedule, think of them as bonus content.

Showcase other people's work and tell them about it
Write a blog in which you share what someone else is doing, involve them, or at least tell them about it and they will share it too, allowing you to access wider networks. It's an easy way to guarantee shares on social media etc.

Encouraging others to share is the only way you'll get any content to go viral. Also, if you say nice things about other people, they'll say nice things about you and that's the key to spreading your message through word of mouth.

Evergreen content
This is content that isn't time sensitive. Include plenty of this in amongst more immediate news, it means you always have content you can re-share that will remain relevant.

Social media and blogging were made for each other
If you are sharing knowledge, imparting wisdom, showcasing other people's work, all of that is social media gold dust.

Remember:

- Blogging is about quality not quantity. It's better to blog less frequently and produce worthwhile content. Aim for once a month initially then build from there, if appropriate.

- Always write what your audience wants to read, not what you want to write (a balance between both is the best solution).

- Find another outlet for your musings if it's not appropriate to your audience. For example: I've kept my blogger 'ideaism.blogspot.co.uk' for my 'Tom Cat's Mewsings'*. It allows me to write what I want without 'contaminating' my business website with inappropriate content.

- Tip: work with a 'blog in hand' so you always have a spare piece of content to use when you're busy.

*Ref: *'Tom Cat Designs' my first art business and sometime artist guise*

Maintaining Momentum

Once you're blogging regularly, it's important to be consistent. It can be challenging when you don't seem to get much feedback on the content you're publishing.

I'm regularly asked to speak, train and present on the nuances of content marketing, with my writer's eye for storytelling, and motivation is always a topic that crops up, along with these common questions - here's four of my Frequently Asked Questions about content marketing:

1. What's the ideal length for a blog post?

There are two schools of thought on this: either, blog little and often, or create long blog articles stuffed with 'keywords'*

Keywords - Words people are likely to type into Google when looking for a product/service like yours.

There is a mounting body of evidence that 3,000+ words articles are popular; but writing a dissertation regularly is a big ask for most of us!

Personally, I believe 500 – 1,000 words is ideal.

Less than 500 and it's difficult to tackle a topic in any meaningful depth, more than 1,000 takes too long to read if you're busy and readers will either skim through or give up part way.

2. How do I know if people are reading my blogs?

Think about your behaviour when you read blogs (including micro-blogging on Facebook) – how often do you comment?

Don't be disheartened if people aren't commenting – most of us don't – it doesn't mean no one is reading what you've written. The only way to know is to look at the stats.

Depending on what platform you use to blog on, make yourself familiar with the analytics; all the major platforms (i.e. WordPress) allow you to monitor your stats.

You can also monitor how many retweets, re-pins, likes and shares you get on social networks.

Another way to see if your content sharing is working is to look at your rank on Google. Are you on the front page (or close to it)?

I've compiled a quick 'Search Engine Optimisation (SEO) Audit Checklist', you'll find it in the templates section at the end of this book.

However, none of this guarantees that people have read the whole blog post, or that they are likely to convert to a customer.

Ultimately, when you post things on social media and blog regularly, these are all small things you can do to raise awareness of your product and/or service – marketing is an inexact science but the secret is 'little and often'.

Keep going, be in lots of places regularly sharing valuable, interesting and entertaining content and the sales will look after themselves.

3. How often should I blog?

There's no right or wrong answer other than to avoid 'feast or famine', and be consistent.

Ultimately, the decision is down to your personal preference; the time you can set aside (or budget you have to pay for writers), what 'the norm' is in your sector, but most importantly: what your customers expect.

If you are new to blogging, build it in gradually. Perhaps start by publishing something once a month, find your rhythm and work on your writing craft. It's far better to write one really well considered thought leadership piece a month than churn out rubbish every day.

Quality not quantity.

As you get used to it, get quicker, more skilled and more confident, aim to publish something weekly.

I'll share some ideas for blog content later in this book.

4. What if we're in a boring industry, what can we talk about?

If your business does something functional and not particularly sexy, it can be tough to come up with interesting things to talk about on a blog and social media. Instead, think outside the scope of what you do and talk about something related to your industry that your customers will be interested in. Develop a theme around that.

Put yourself in your customers' shoes. Ask yourself why they buy your products/services? How can you 'edu-tain' (educate + entertain) them about your business?

Here's a few examples and suggestions for themes for content to create and share for businesses that aren't always easy to get excited about:

- Insurance: The stupid and frivolous insurance claims people make

- Health & Safety: Ridiculous examples of health & safety or tackle some H&S facts and fiction (i.e. Do kids need to wear safety googles when playing conkers?)

- Picture framing: Colour matching, picture hanging tips and arrangements, unusual things people put in picture frames, tips to mount your images etc.

Bringing It To Life

I've talked a lot about storytelling, and developing a compelling narrative is essential to draw in the curious, peak their interest and 'move them' to respond to your 'call to action'. A storyteller has many tools in our wonderfully versatile language we use to elicit different reactions.

Remember: 'we react, we act'. Make them react, then give them something to act on (a Call to Action).

If you've ever been to any business workshops or events the chances are that at some point someone has asked you "What's your USP?" (Unique Selling Point).

I've always hated that question. Not because I couldn't fudge some satisfactory answer to it, but because it's meaningless.

Unless you've invented something ground-breaking, most of us can't honestly say that our business and the work we do is completely unique. It's hard to even say we do things in a unique way; just by the law of averages and attrition, the chances are, someone else, somewhere in the world, does what you do and does it in a similar way.

The only thing you can absolutely, 100% guarantee, that's unique about your business is YOU; and the thing that makes you YOU is your STORY.

No two people's stories are ever the same; even siblings will remember different things that impacted their lives, moments of joy and moments of despair. If you ever recount a childhood memory with a sibling, they will probably remember something different to you, because we all have different ways of perceiving things.

Those three letters U S P have been so overused in business now they have become a cliché; but when we ask someone that, what are we really asking?

We want to know why X business is different to Y business, when on the face of it they seem to do the same thing.

Perhaps DSP (Different Selling Point) is more accurate? Perhaps we should be asking: "What's your DSP?" At least that means something?

But it's more than that, it's your SSP - your Story Selling Point - that will keep people curious.

A truly compelling story will provoke an emotional reaction from us. Whether the story makes us laugh, makes us cry, makes us empathise and feel as though the story teller is speaking directly to our own hearts - if we react, we act.

A good story has a character, an action and a resolution; a great story has heroes and villains, it has conflict, it has us rooting for the hero, it has thrills and spills and - I know it's a cheesy - but it has a happy ending, where our protagonist improves or grows themselves in some way (beat the bad guys, save the world).

The problem with both USP and DSP is that both are about you and your business, rather than the people that turn your brilliant idea into an actual business – your customers.

The story of your business is not just a sequence of events that got you from idea to market - customers want to know what's at the heart of your business.

What compels you? What moves you? What was it that sent you down the path you find yourself on and where are your going from here? Was there a single inciting incident somewhere in your past that motivated, inspired, scared or encouraged you?

That's the story of your business, and the key to finding your Story Selling Point (SSP) to draw in the curious, start a conversation and build the relationships so customers choose you and not an alternative service.

So what's the story of your business? What's your SSP?

In the templates section you will find a short questionnaire to help you get to the heart and soul of your business. There are no right or wrong answers, complete it as honestly as you can and use it as the basis for the 'tone' you set for your blog.

Tone

The 'tone' you choose to write in should resonate with your audience. Tone is a powerful writing tool to convey the story, and a big part of your identity. We recognise 'voices'.

Readers of prolific authors, such as Stephen King, will immediately recognise the tone he writes in. In the same way you can spot a Van Gogh painting or a David Hockney. Or a film directed by Michael Mann or JJ Abrams. You can hear a song and know immediately that it's a U2 song.

Music, art, film, words, these are all ways to communicate our voice. We each have a particular 'style' – that's part of your 'brand'.

Are there words and phrases you use a lot? What are people used to hearing you say? Do you have a particular style? Perhaps your style is tongue in cheek? Dryly humourous? Formal or informal? All this forms the tone that you want to convey in your writing making you instantly recognisable, it's what makes you authentic.

If you are in a sector that is dominated by formal communication and jargon, perhaps your SSP is that you speak to people differently?

The 'voice' you use is just as much a part of your story as the action within it.

The Story Arc

How stories are structured is an enormous subject and there are mountains of research and information on the topic, I'm not about to tackle that in this short book, but I will distill it down to some basics.

A story must have a beginning, a middle and an end.

Readers like a nice tidy loop, it's satisfying.

Cliffhangers work well in fiction; the audience is hungry to see how it ends and they want to feel satisfaction from investing time, energy and emotion in that story. Cliffhangers are a great way to get people hooked in, but it needs to conclude at some point, otherwise the audience will get frustrated and lose patience.

The basic formula for a story is:

Character + conflict = story

We meet a character (it doesn't necessarily have to be a person) we get to know them and empathise with them, then there is some form of conflict.

Conflict can be action, it can involve outside intervention, or it can be an internal struggle. We see the stakes raised, we follow the character as they fight the conflict and we experience some sort of resolution, or at the very least, a fundamental change in that character.

It's called an 'arc' because if you were to plot this build up, action then resolution on a chart it would look like a 'normal distribution curve', it would be an 'arc' shape.

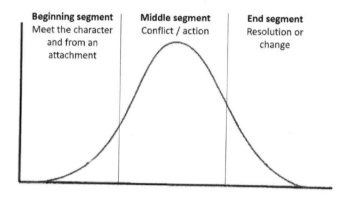

Point of View

There are three points of view you could write from:

1. First Person = I did this
2. Second Person = You are doing this
3. Third Person = He / She did this

Different viewpoints will work in different situations.

In this book, I'm using a mix of first and second person. I'm talking about 'me' and 'my' experience, then referring to 'you', enabling you to put yourself in my shoes and relate the contents of this book to your own business.

In my fiction novels, The Sheridan and Blake Adventure Series, I write predominantly in the third person. I do this because the series is built around a puzzle, gradually solved by a selection of characters working with and against each other. I put my reader in the heads of each of those characters, allowing them to immerse themselves in the story from every angle and understand the motivations of each of those characters.

If my books involved one central character, I would be more likely to write in the first person - as the reader you live the story through the perspective of that protagonist.

In non-fiction, a mix of first and second person is the most common way to address your readers, it's the most assertive and persuasive in this context.

You will be writing about you in your business, and to create that personal touch, most of your writing will be from a first person context. You are placing yourself at the centre of the narrative, you are the protagonist in the story of your business.

Tenses

The English language is made up of a complex mix of tenses that native speakers use instinctively. Anyone who has studied the language in any depth, for example, when studying for a TEFL (Teaching English as a Foreign Language) qualification, will know we structure conversation using a combination of tenses that change the meaning, impact and action of the verb.

This isn't an English language book, and I'm not going to explore these in detail, but again, understanding the basics can really lift the way you communicate in writing. The tenses fall into three categories:

1. Past (already happened)
2. Present (happening right now)
3. Continuous (continuing to happen into the future)

If you want to convey something that has already happened, you would use a 'past tense'. For example:

"I have been to the shop"

If you are communicating something happening right now you would use a 'present tense'. For example:

"I go to the shop"

If you are communicating something that has started happening and is continuing to happen you will use 'continuous' tense i.e.: add 'ing' to the verb. For example:

"I am going to the shop"

In writing, play around with the points of view you use and the tenses.

Using fewer words can give the writing more 'impact', more words make it more 'passive'. This can be useful in different contexts depending on what reaction you want to provoke from the receiver.

For example, if you are writing something and want to appease the receiver in some way, you may use more words, make it past tense to be more passive in your tone.

If you are writing something that needs to convey an impact and draw people along with your momentum, using a combination of present and continuous tenses will make the reader feel like they are in the thick of the action and then continue to follow it.

Here's some examples of how changing the tense and focus can change the 'feel' of a sentence:

"I went to the shop, when I found" (first person, past)

"You go to the shop and discover" (second person, present)

"She was going to the shop, when she found" (third person, past continuous)

"I'm going into the shop and I discover" (first person, present continuous)

You can also choose more powerful descriptive words to reinforce it, in this example, substituting 'found' with 'discover'.

Top writing tips:

- The best writing says a lot with as few words as possible
- Use simple words, avoid long words and jargon
- Experiment with tenses, tone and point of view - but be careful to stay consistent within a sentence – avoid 'head hopping' and 'time hopping'.
- Cut unnecessary words. For example, 'starting to' – is it happening or not? *"She was starting to walk"* becomes: *"She walked"*
- Always get your work proof read. When we proof read our own work, we miss mistakes we didn't realise we were making and our brain reads what it thinks it's written.
- Remember, criticism is just a chance to improve. Don't take it personally, use it to do better next time. Ask people what's wrong with your writing, not just what's good about it.

Anatomy of an Effective Blog Post

A blog post that grabs attention, keeps the reader engaged and allows them to catalogue that post for future reference, has several features in common:

- Well written and proof read (I offer a proof reading subscription service)

- At least 1 good quality, relevant, image, making the post 'pinnable' and breaking up the text

- An image with a text overlay is more likely to be shared on social media – put the title of the post on a relevant image for maximum impact

- Social Media sharing buttons

- An appealing headline/title

- Plenty of white space

- Bullet points and lists are more likely to be shared

- A beginning, middle and end

- A call to action

- Filled with SEO Keywords (words that people might search for in Google to find it) and relevant 'tags' added (use the tools in your blog software to emphasis these keywords by tagging them).

- Hyperlinks. Link words in the content naturally to other pages on your website and to other websites. These crosslinks boost SEO

Be Inspired

Keeping your content fresh and absorbing requires imagination, motivation, inspiration and dedication.

Here's my list of 120 blog ideas to get you started and keep you going:

1. List posts i.e. Bucket list
2. Top Tips posts
3. Be interviewed
4. Interview an expert
5. Interview a celebrity
6. Interview a customer
7. Testimonials
8. Case Studies
9. Review podcasts
10. Create and share images of quotations
11. Review books (use an affiliate link to monetize)
12. Your take on an inspirational quote
13. Share the best TED talks in your sector
14. Best Podcasts in your sector
15. Product reviews (these can earn you money or get you freebies)
16. List of influencers to follow on Social Media and why (let them know for maximum shares)
17. List your goals for the coming year – follow up after 6 & 12 months
18. Track progress i.e. weekly roundup, etc.
19. Comment on a relevant news story
20. Review new technology
21. Test new technology (this can get you freebies)
22. Video blog (Vlog)
23. Short stories
24. Host a guest post
25. Run a competition
26. Create a quiz
27. List useful YouTube videos on a topic
28. Infographics
29. Conduct a survey. Share results later
30. Share music playlists to inspire different activities

31. Comment on current affairs that are relevant
32. Share #'s list for your subject/sector
33. Review a destination
34. Comment/review seminar or workshop
35. The good, the bad and the ugly of…
36. Top 10 tips for…
37. Then and now comparisons
38. What #'s are trending? Choose one that inspires an idea
39. Lessons from fictional characters
40. Links to useful blogs about a topic
41. Share some useful online tools/apps
42. Extract from an eBook and sell the book at the end
43. Discuss a thought provoking article
44. Refute someone else's article
45. Expand on someone else's article
46. Review a local business (tell them)
47. Compare and contrast businesses i.e. Café's to work in
48. Publicly thank someone
49. Pictures from an event
50. Create tutorial/ how to
51. Review tutorials/how to
52. Critique someone else's work
53. Show 'behind the scenes'
54. Talk about your perfect day
55. Talk about your typical day
56. Share your dreams/vision for the future
57. Share the best lesson you've learned and expand
58. Ask several people a question and share responses
59. FAQ's (Frequently Asked Questions)
60. SAQ's (Should Ask Questions)
61. Share 'Best of'
62. Write an open letter about an important issue
63. Share a challenge you faced and how you overcame it
64. Ask for feedback i.e. on 2 images
65. Share a checklist i.e. Blog sharing checklist
66. List favourite websites/blogs
67. List favourite shops and why (possibly be paid for this)
68. Write a tribute to someone who's inspired you
69. List of self-help books in your topic
70. Write a poem
71. Share your research
72. Definitions – define a concept in detail
73. Ultimate guides

74. Write a series of pieces on a topic (later, sell it as an eBook)
75. Manifesto – your values, beliefs
76. Diary entry post
77. Predictions
78. Reaction to someone else's content
79. Create a list of common mistakes
80. Do's and Don'ts
81. Audio post
82. Take part in a blog tour
83. Bust popular myths
84. Music playlist for particular moods or topics
85. Review magazines
86. Share your to do list
87. A list of blog post ideas!
88. List great gift ideas (possibly get freebies)
89. List fictional heroes and heroines and why
90. If you could have dinner with anyone who would it be?
91. Childhood memory and how it's influenced you
92. Post a philosophical question and invite responses
93. Share inspiring images
94. Share inspiring words
95. Pros and Cons lists
96. Dictionary style definitions – why not even make them satirical
97. Share some jokes
98. List relevant competitions
99. A 'sarcastic anti-post'
100. That day in history - what happened and how things have changed/not changed
101. Revisit an old blog post - expand your argument or update it
102. Share latest research in your sector and comment
103. Share stats in your sector and comment
104. Repurpose an old blog into a video, podcast, info graphic, image etc. (more on this later)
105. Recount the X best things from your week
106. Write about X things you'd do differently if had a second chance
107. Tell a secret about yourself
108. Create and summarise an in depth guide (sell the eBook)
109. Talk about your successes and failures
110. Share your conspiracy theories
111. Disprove an accepted theory
112. A memorial for someone/something lost – satirical or serious
113. If you won the lottery what would you do?
114. List common mistake in your subject area

115. Feature a 'fan' and dedicate a post to them
116. Host a live event i.e. Webinar
117. Offer a freebie
118. Rant about something
119. Create a comic strip to illustrate a serious point
120. What would you do if you had a time machine?

Re-use and Recycle

Once you are blogging regularly, over time you will build up a library of content. This knowledge has value and can therefore add value to the portfolio of your business.

Every time you write a piece of content you're creating something new, something with the potential to use over and over again.

I recently told a client I was lazy. He gave me a crooked look and said; "Way to sell yourself, Amy?"

…I'm lazy because: I like to have simple systems and processes in place so I can get stuff done, quickly and effectively, leaving room in my day to do what I enjoy. There's no sense in constantly reinventing the wheel. I want to do something once then re-use, re-purpose and recycle it (without being repetitive).

When you create a new piece of content, look for opportunities to use that knowledge in different ways. Here are 15 ways to make the most out of that piece of content:

It's not just a blog post, it can also be…

1. Workshop handouts
2. The basis of a face to face workshop
3. A flow chart
4. Built into an online course
5. Visually represented as an infographic
6. Recorded as a podcast
7. Presented in video form
8. Turned into a cartoon
9. A printable
10. Made into a quiz
11. Gamified (turned into a game)

12. Revisited and referenced into an updated post
13. Used as a checklist
14. Presentation slides to deliver as a talk
15. Expanded on to form the basis of an eBook. I've done this with 'Authorpreneur Almanac' (and this book to a certain degree).

Eyes On

So you've crafted this wonderful piece of writing, with a powerful call to action and some gorgeous images.

Now what? How do you get eyes on it?

- **SEO**
  A well written blog post will be filled with relevant keywords and will be found more easily with an organic Google search

- **Newsletter**
  Add the blog post or repurpose it to include in your newsletter

- **Email**
  Email the link to your contacts list

- **Marketing Materials**
  Include your website, the location of your blog, on all of your marketing materials

- **Email Signature**
  Include your blog link on your email signature

- **Networking**
  Tell people you meet about the content when it comes up in conversation, refer to it at events and presentations, etc.

- **Social Sharing Sites**
  Add the link to StumbleUpon and if relevant, add it to Reddit

Social Media
Twitter and Pinterest are the biggest drivers of traffic to my website

- Tweet it immediately
- Use tools like Hootesuite/Buffer/Tweetdeck to schedule in multiple tweets over the course of the next few weeks and months, varying the tweet and the hashtags
- @Mention anyone you refer to in the blog with a message, i.e. '@whoever put a shout out for you on my latest blog URLlink'
- Pinterest: Pin all of the images from the blog with different descriptive text to multiple boards of your own and also on group boards
- Share the link on Linked In
- Republish the blog on Linked In Pulse
- Share in relevant Linked In groups
- Direct message people that you know will be interested in the content via Twitter, Facebook, Linked In, etc.
- Add an update on Google+
- If there is a video, load it to YouTube first then embed it onto your blog. Make sure you include a detailed, keyword filled description with the video on YouTube (YouTube is the second biggest search engine after Google)
- Facebook: Share on your business pages. Share in relevant groups you are a member of. Share on your personal timeline if appropriate. Consider paying for a boost or an advert.

(For more tips and ideas to make better use of Social Media, get my 'Operation Author: Let's Get Social' eBook.)

Action Templates

Here's the homework...

This is your business, your blog, you are in control of it.

These templates are to help you make the most of the information in this book.

If you would like to discuss the writing challenges within your business in specific detail, contact me through the website for a no obligation free ½ hour phone or Skype consultation.

Good luck. You can write your way to success!

www.AmyMorse.co.uk

SEO Checklist

> What words would my customers use to search for my product or service? (These are 'keywords' and 'long links'):

Have I written descriptions for my images? _____

Have I crosslinked to other parts of my website? _____

Do I have my Social Media links on my website? _____

Have I added my website to my Social Media Profiles? _____

Have I included keywords in content? _____

Do all the links work? _____

Do I have active social sharing links? _____

Do I have clear and concise headings on my pages? _____
(<H1> Primary heading, <H2> Secondary heading)

Useful SEO reference sites:

- https://moz.com/
- http://searchengineland.com/

The Story of Your Business, Questionnaire

Answer these 18 questions as fully and honestly as you can. There are no right or wrong answers, this is about drawing out the soul of your business so you can share your story with the world.

1. Why did you become self-employed?
2. Why did you decide to do what you're doing?
3. Why is now the right time for you to be in business?
4. What would you do with yourself if you didn't have to work?
5. What's the most important thing in your life?
6. What really makes you smile from the inside out?
7. What are you insanely passionate about?
8. What's the best thing you've ever done?
9. What achievement are you most proud of?
10. What advice would you give to your 16-year-old self?
11. Where do you want to be in 5 years' time?
12. What makes your heart sing?
13. Is this your first business? How has it evolved and what's the journey been like?
14. Is there one thing you wish someone had told you before you went into business?
15. Is there one piece of advice you would give to someone else starting a business?
16. Who do you serve? Be specific, think of everyone your business impacts (not just customers)

17. How do you want the world to see your business?

18. What would you like people to say about you and your business?

Now put your responses on an email to me and we'll book a FREE phone or Skype consultation to discover the story behind your business and how I can help you tell it in your own words.

Email: Amy@AmyMorse.co.uk

More Books

Amy Morse has published two other non-fiction eBooks to date. You can find these on Amazon:

- Operation Author: Let's Get Social

- Authorpreneur Almanac: 52 Adventures in Writing and Entrepreneurship

Amy also publishes fiction books in her maiden name, Amy C Fitzjohn.

The Sheridan and Blake Adventure Series is out now on Amazon.

- Book 1:   The Bronze Box

- Book 2:   Solomon's Secrets

- Book 3:   Gabriel's Game
             Part 1, The White Queen
             Part 2, The Black Knight

About the Author

Amy Morse was born as Amy C Fitzjohn in Swansea in 1976. Growing up in the East Midlands and later in the Westcountry, she now lives in the eclectic city of Bristol UK with her husband.

She published her first fiction novel, The Bronze Box, as Amy C Fitzjohn in 2013 and has gone on to write further fiction novels.

Amy's background has been in skills training, business support and writing, she writes non-fiction books as Amy Morse. She now works with small businesses to help them tell their stories better in their own words and write their way to success.

Look out for further non-fiction titles from Amy Morse:

> www.AmyMorse.co.uk

and for fiction works from this promising emerging author, Amy C Fitzjohn:

> www.AmyCFitzjohn.co.uk

Follow link and engage with Amy on Social Media:

Twitter: @AmyMorse_Writer
Facebook.com/AmyMorseAuthorpreneur
Facebook.com/AmyCFitzjohn
Pinterest: AmyMorse187

Made in the USA
Charleston, SC
14 August 2016